All Your Dead Were Civilized
and other misheard lyrics

Selected prose and poetry
from 2010 and 2011

a collection by
Ace Edmonds

© Copyright Ace Edmonds 2010-2011

It's Not Raining

you shot me, now I'm dying,
but there's too much left to say.
please don't poke me, please don't prod me,
I'm disrespected anyway.

you hit me, now I'm fading,
the world is turning grey;
I'm falling, Lord, I'm falling...
I don't want to die today.

I'm losing all my memories,
I'm losing my own name,
I'm losing my future...
shouldn't there be rain?

                18 November 2010

When The Gods Stop Crying

I can see them spinning, the world sifting, shifting, and when the night grows so long, I can do nothing but try to add a light into this world.

Climb to the top of my lighthouse, and find the shining light. Try to climb down, and the stairs just go 'round and 'round. It may be a paradox or just trick of the mind. I could pinch you, but even in a dream you'd feel it. You know you climbed these stairs and made it to the top, but to descend... these are not the same stairs.

If you're tired, I left snacks under the lamp for you, and maybe more than that. There's a dumbwaiter in the wall, and it will take more than your leftovers. As the doors close, it hardly feels like a dumbwaiter at all, as it plummets past depths you never could have reach on those stairs. You know it's descending, but there's no lurch in your stomach: you can breathe, you can swallow. It feels so real but some sensation is missing: the discomfort.

What is that in your pocket? I've never seen it before, and as you pull it out, I feel a strange presence, one that wasn't here before. What is that in your hand? I didn't create it, so you must have brought it with you. It's so bright, and I can't touch it, but I want it gone.

You toss it up in the air, and I reach out my fingers to catch it, but it just slips through my fingers as if I'm not really here. I'm worried it might taint my design, and you reach out your hand to catch it, but it just hangs there, spinning still but slowing, until there's a small full moon shining down on you.

A smirk, and you reach up for it again, and it becomes a coin once more, and this time I see her face, her name, in a glimpse before you slip it back into your pocket. Lady Liberty.

The doors open, and you're surprised. Good, I like that. You didn't notice when the elevator stopped descending, but you aren't startled when you step out of the old tree and into the broad field. I'm disappointed.

A rope snaps above your head, and you glance upward into the tree suddenly. A man hangs there, and I know I'm still in control. I know his face, since it's not much different from my own, though aged and wizened beyond what you ever perceived in my own.

Blood drips from a gaping hole in his side, and it slides down the tree, but he still breathes. You turn away, and look across the plain, though I wish you would return to him, you have places to go, miles before you sleep.

A farmhouse is on the other side of the plain of gold, wheat waving at you despite no breeze, but neither of us is bothered by this phenomenon. You start toward the farmhouse.

You're going to reach it faster than you think, for as lovingly as I built this landscape, even I can appreciate it for only so long. But, if you turn back to return to the tree, you will find the same trial as the staircase in the lighthouse. Still, there's no reason to try that: the farmhouse has all the answers you'll ever need.

The paint, once red, is peeling, and the wood is long dead and dark beneath, but the door opens without a squeak. A faint smell of long gone manure permeates the building, but it's not uncomfortably strong.

In one of the stalls, third from the back on the left, if I remember correctly, there's someone I want you to meet. Yes, there she is.

You'll perceive her as them, but it doesn't make any difference to what she is. She holds a cup while they lean over a trough, but they're both filled with the same water.

There's no reflection, but then, you weren't expecting one. OAR starts playing in your ears, and you dip your fingers into the water. She-They protest as you bring your fingers to your lips.

21 August 2010

My Cup Runneth Over

whisper through the trees
and whisper throu-ough me,
whisper in my mind,
take the gale, take the grind,
and the wind will set you free.

hold your ground and hold the sky,
hold the chalice and the rye,
(to the Goddess I do make
and worship She will take;
all others need not apply)

30 November 2010

Wrote Your Own Rules

shake your palm, upside down
    you are trapped in the dream:
    you are more than you seem.
    you have stories and games
    just waiting to play,
    but you must remember what it means.

    you're diving into your dreams
        nothing is real,
        nothing will stay,
        nothing you promised
        will ever come my way.
    where everything is more than it seems;
        nothing will stay
        but it grows in the night,
        something comes this way,
        and I must make it right.
    someone telling stories, trapped in games
        we're growing in the night,
        our beauty, our lives,
        we must make it right...
        it's coming, our time.
    trapped and forced to join and play
        our beauty builds life,
        but we must agree to live.
        it's coming, our time,
        to grow, remember, decide.
    and you can't remember what it means...

we must decide to live,
for everything we promised.
we're growing and deciding...
Wake Up, and know it is real.

you're not trapped in the dream:
you are more than you seem.
you have stories and games
just waiting to play,
but you will remember what it means.
let the dice fall so you can play

8 December 2010

Weightless

pierce me where it hurts the most,
get in hard and get in close,
break my darkness with your light.
at long last everything will be alright.

take my blessings with the moon,
she's my inheritance, she'll be here soon;
light up my world with your heart
and my world won't fall apart.

lift me, raise me, to your dais high,
I cannot fall once I touch the sky.

                    21 December 2010

We're Only Caterpillars

come dance along with butterflies,
like my fingers on your back;
come dance and metamorphosize
upon this unlit track.

come and dance and follow me
deeper into these trees;
there's a place in here I hold dear,
it's in you and it's in me.

come and glow with lightning bugs,
join nature in it's place;
leave all of civilisation behind,
show the Goddess your true face.

    16 December 2010

We Are Alien

when the waters overcome
but can barely wash away,
all the buildings never crumbled,
all the garbage there to stay,..

when the future falls behind
and our natures do regress,
alien mysteries unfold,
unbidden from the past.

                    14 Oct 2010

Skipping Stones

spread your wings and fly so high
dance dance dance upon the sky,
kiss the stars. no, kiss my star...
I'll catch you if you fall too far.

lightning from my fingers and thunder in my toes,
skipping across the heavens like a pond's well tossed
    stones.

30 November 2010

New-Fashioned, Not Old

you can be my hourglass
in this digital age,
gotta keep on turning turning
so you're always on my page.

you can be my fission
in this nuclear age,
show me how we multiply
and I'll open up your cage.

you can be my magic
in this scientific age,
have free reign with my wand
and we'll move on to the next stage.

                5 January 2011

More Than Just An Audience

sit where I can see you,
don't dare turn away.
you've got me where you want me:
wouldn't you rather stay?

>5 January 2011

I'd Rather Dream Forever Than Wake Up Without You

this is the door into summer,
though spring is already here,
dearest door into summer,
I will hold you dear.

this is the door of the dream realm
where everything is real;
I can fly, I can live,
I can sleep, I can feel.

this is the door into tomorrow,
yesterday is back a little ways,
both are locked and keyless,
both want us to stay:

who needs a door to anywhere,
when all I want is right here.
I've no need to awaken,
you are my summer all year.

                6 January 2011

All Natural, Chemical Free

give me a book to hold the world in,
to grow the stories that I tell,
a tree nourished by my words:
fertilizer I make myself.

>21 December 2010

Even If I Were Blind

you can close your eyes and look away
but you can't discount the words I say.
you can refuse to listen, refuse to hear,
you can decline to acknowledge I'm standing
    there,
but you're too colorful to be painted in grey.

      22 December 2010

Gamemaster Wears No Nametag

you can try to hide your face,
but I still know who you are;
you crept down my back stairwell
thinking you set off no alarm,

but I know who you work for
and I know the details of your past.
I know what your game is
and I know You. Won't. Last.

                    6 December 2010

<u>Stop Pretending</u>

you can pose
and prosper.

you can moue
and stay mute.

you can huddle,
unhumble.

you can cut
something cute.

you can pretend
you're too good

for the likes
of little me.

you will stumble
you will stutter

when I break away
free.

                22 December 2010

How We March

I don't know what you've been told
    I don't know what you've been told
but the future won't unfold
    but the future won't unfold
if you don't stand and let if go
    if you don't stand and let if go
open your mind and let it grow
    open your mind and let it grow

29 December 2010

<u>Anywhere But Here</u>

take me away to somewhere,
wherever you will be.
I'll leave behind my bloodkin
to make my family.

fly with me away, anywhere,
give me walls, a roof, a floor.
I'll be spoiled while I have you
and won't need any more.

drift with me away, somewhere,
float to the ends of the seas,
    'til the water merges with the sun,
    'til you and I become just one,
to wherever we can breathe.

              11 December 2010

Together We'll Win Out

I'll be your bridge tonight,
if you'll be my scarlet robe;
I'll connect us as we dance,
you'll wrap me head to toe.

I'll be the rhythm of your heart,
if you'll keep pounding to the beat;
I'll sing you a new melody,
you'll find me twice as sweet.

I'll glow in your darkness,
if you'll save me from the light;
I'll drown out all the ugly stars,
you'll hold me with everlasting might.

13 April 2010

A Chance Game

you can toss me
you can push me
you can throw me away
you can punish
you can torture
you can rue my every day
you can bully
you can tease
you can watch me tally the days
til it's over
til it's over
til I go my own way.

          30 November 2010

Saved In Another Timeline

a butterfly hit my windshield,
driving home this very night,
squandered all that beauty
impacting in my sight.

a butterfly flew right by me,
and I biked on down the road,
pumping my pedals with my strength,
caught by my sight alone.

9 April 2010

Ambush?

sneak up behind us
like you're barely even there,
we're caught up in our watching,
caught completely unaware.

you blend into no shadows,
stand brightly in the sun,
walk on heavy iron feet,
walk when you could have run.

maybe we'll turn and catch you,
maybe it'll be too late,
maybe we're doomed to die today
or maybe we're the bait.

                7 April 2010

White Mistress

The leaves were already turning, and it felt too soon, like spring had just left and summer should still be in full bloom. But no, the leaves were turning, and beginning to fall.

I stumbled through the woods to find my resting ground, where I would lie through the snow and dream of spring rains; where I would sleep through the cold and garb myself in my own warmth and the muted warmth of the earth rising below me; when I came across winter's own mistress. The cold was always harsh to me, leaving my joints aching and begging for relief, but she was beautiful. My heart whispered sweet nothings that fell and froze on unhearing ears.

I found I could not move, crouched in the shadows of a nearly bare bush. She was simply too alluring. As sunlight stabbed down into the clearing, shifting and weaving about herself, I realized she was not alone.

Two snow-white peacocks wove in the darkness of the woods and glowing light of the clearing around her. Their brightness against my world of darkness left spots on my vision, until all I could see were their trails.

Slowly again, the spots faded and no one and nothing danced before me. My joints groaned in pain, and I crawled carefully forward. Above, flakes of snow were beginning to fall. I stretched again, before hurrying on my way.

<u>All Your Dead Were Civilized</u>

all your dead were civilized,
and they brought my own to me.
I taught them how to farm the land
between here and manido-aki.

all my dead were reminded
of all they were to me;
I saved them from their punishment,
from all of eternity.

all my dead are dying,
gave all that they could give,
tilled the fields of manna:
so I alone could live.

      11 January 2011

Not Now, Not Tonight

I don't need any windows
since I've got my mind inside,
it takes me for the wildest,
endless ride.

I don't need to meet you,
when I already know you through,
for here, my imagination,
has taken over for you.

I don't need any lyrics,
I've already supplied the melody,
and the spirit that moves
is here inside of me.

>   5 July 2010

Learning To Understand

butterflies in my eye
and caterpillars in my hand,
landing on me,
trusting me,
in ways I don't understand.

speckles in my cornea
and light streaming from my eye,
I trust I'll know
how to live with the glow,
and take everything else in stride.

                9 November 2010

To Thank You Properly

spread your arms open wide
so I may find shelter inside;
let me huddle and grow warm,
let me find shelter from the storm,
and then I'll continue on my way.

grow with the stories I tell,
teeth chattering against my will;
staying awake with my voice
since freezing asleep is not my choice...
perhaps I'll return some day

                8 January 2011

Free

I can see all I need to see,
trapped here in this room with me,
locked away behind the screen:
every thing that makes me free.

          29 November 2010

When The Gods Stop Burning

The wind whipped the few remaining leaves as they strained on their buds and branches. The sky was as dark as a cloudy midsummer's twilight, but you knew those weren't clouds. The smell of ash stung in your mouth and nose.

Above you, that tree, which once held the body of a man, was still stained with his blood, showing deep and black in the darkness. The field before you was long since plowed and replanted and replowed, the furrows long and deep and leeched of nutrients. Across that long field that once waved brilliant golden strands sat a smoking ruin.

As you approach, the ash will sting your eyes and stain your clothes. You will stand there, watching the world smolder.

There's clearly nothing left for you here, as the landscape blends into the grey sky, but something keeps pulling you back. Turn slowly in a circle, and remember the life this place held in your last visit, now long past. We know your curiosity would get the better of you, and while your hands are jammed into your pockets and absently playing with their meager contents, you don't pull out the silver Liberty dollar. When you remove your hands, instead its familiar weigh still presses against you thigh through the thin cloth.

You push what remains of the door aside as you step into the farmhouse. The walls are all but gone and the visible foundation stones are burned as black as the stain on the tree. The stalls are gone, marked only by the metal braces that held the gates, now fallen to the packed-earth floor.

    Counting your paces more carefully than the stalls, you return to where you think the women sat. In truth, you're one stall short, but that doesn't matter. There's nothing there: no walls, no women, no water.

    You can run from these ruins but they'll still haunt you; the stains will never come off your clothes, off your skin, and the smell of ash will always bring all these images, unbidden, back to your mind.

28 September 2010

The Fallen Have Dreams Too

I caught death staring at me.
He was amazed at all that I could see.
I caught death staring at me;
I stared him down so he could see
everything he wished I could be.

                21 December 2010